1980

The Stowe-Day Foundation was established and endowed by the late Katharine Seymour Day, a grandniece of Harriet Beecher Stowe. It is located on Nook Farm, the famous nineteenth-century neighborhood in which Harriet Beecher Stowe, Mark Twain, Isabella Beecher Hooker, Charles Dudley Warner, William Gillette, and other notables lived.

The Stowe-Day Foundation owns and maintains the Harriet Beecher Stowe House, 73 Forest Street, Hartford, Connecticut, and The Stowe-Day Library, 77 Forest Street. The Library contains over 15,000 volumes, 6,000 pamphlets, and 100,000 manuscript items — all fully catalogued. The basic collections focus upon the architecture, the decorative arts, the history, the literature, and the woman suffrage movement of the nineteenth century.

The publications of The Stowe-Day Foundation reflect the interests of the Library. A recent catalogue is available by writing.

Also by Ellen Moers
 Literary Women
 Two Dreisers
 The Dandy: Brummell to Beerbohm

Harriet Beecher Stowe
and
American Literature

Harriet Beecher Stowe
and
American Literature

Ellen Moers

The Stowe-Day Foundation
77 Forest Street
Hartford, Connecticut
1978

Library of Congress Cataloging in Publication Data

Moers, Ellen, 1928-
  Harriet Beecher Stowe and American literature.

  "A note on Mark Twain and Harriet Beecher Stowe": p.
  Includes bibliographical references.
  1. Stowe, Harriet Elizabeth Beecher, 1811-1896 — Addresses, essays,
lectures. 2. Stowe, Harriet Elizabeth Beecher, 1811-1896. Uncle Tom's
cabin. 3. Slavery in the United States in literature — Addresses, essays,
lectures. 4. American fiction — 19th century — History and criticism —
Addresses, essays, lectures. 5. Clemens, Samuel Langhorne, 1835-1910 —
Addresses, essays, lectures. 6. Authors, American — 19th century —
Biography — Addresses, essays, lectures.

I. Title
PS2956.M6   813'.3   78-4149
ISBN 0-917482-15-8

Library of Congress Catalog Card Number 78-4149
ISBN 0-917482-15-8

Endpaper design from the wallpaper seen in an 1886 photograph of the front
parlor of the Harriet Beecher Stowe House, Hartford, Connecticut. Repro-
duced exclusively for The Stowe-Day Foundation.

Photographic credits

All photographs, unless otherwise cited, are by courtesy of The Stowe-Day Foundation.

The illustrations by George Cruikshank, 1792-1878, on pp. 5, 6, 9, 14, 17, 19, 24, appeared in the first English edition of *Uncle Tom's Cabin*, London: J. Cassell, 1852.

Photographs appearing on the cover and on pp. 23, 38, 42, 45, have never been published.

Photograph of Frederick Douglass is by courtesy of the National Portrait Gallery, Smithsonian Institution, Washington, D.C.

Photographic prints by Terry Harlow.

Cover photograph: Harriet Beecher Stowe, c. 1869-1872, New York City.

The book that moved me most ... was then beginning to move the whole world more than any other book has moved it. I read it as it came out week after week in the old National Era, *and I broke my heart over* Uncle Tom's Cabin, *as every one else did. ... I felt its greatness when I read it first, and as often as I have read it since, I have seen more and more clearly that it was a very great novel ... still perhaps our chief fiction. ...*

William Dean Howells

If I were required to point out in modern art the models of each of these kinds of art, I should point, as to models of a higher art, which arises from the love of God and of our neighbour, in the sphere of literature, to Schiller's Robbers; *from the moderns, to Hugo's* Les Pauvres Gens *and to his* Les Misérables; *to Dickens's stories and novels,* Tale of Two Cities, Chimes, *and others, to* Uncle Tom's Cabin, *to Dostoévski, especially his* Dead House, *to George Eliot's* Adam Bede.

Tolstoi

... if we are to take seriously the literature of the South, from Mark Twain to Faulkner, and if we are to accept that our own age shows the true flowering of the novel of protest, we cannot afford to neglect Mrs. Stowe, who was the mother of both. ... Uncle Tom's Cabin *has been chiefly neglected — in our own age — because it is hard to accept that an instrument of historical change should also be a work of art. ... If the book is to mean anything now, a good deal of the meaning must reside in the art.*

Anthony Burgess

Harriet Beecher Stowe and American Literature was delivered to the Friends of The Harriet Beecher Stowe House and Research Library in Hartford, Connecticut, in November 1976.

Harriet Beecher Stowe
and
American Literature

WHEN I first learned, about a dozen years ago, that Mark Twain lived next door to Harriet Beecher Stowe in the 1870s and 1880s, I said at once to myself — "So! *that* explains why Mark Twain wrote *Huckleberry Finn*! That explains why some twenty years after Emancipation Mark Twain wrote a Mississippi River book about a boy helping a fugitive slave to escape."

This reaction of mine is, I am quite aware, an eccentric one, for in America we are not in the habit of speculating on the literary consequences of *Uncle Tom's Cabin,* only the historical. We think of *Uncle Tom's Cabin* as belonging to American history — and *Huckleberry Finn* to American literature. My intention is to put *Uncle Tom's Cabin* back in American literature where it belongs, for I think it is a great novel. Turgenev, Victor Hugo, George Eliot, Heine, George Sand, Tolstoi, Macaulay were of much the same opinion, still commonplace in Europe, where *Uncle Tom's Cabin* remains a world classic everyone is expected to have read.[1] But in this country Harriet Beecher Stowe's novel has been more of an embarrassment than a resource to professors of our literature. It doesn't fit; it upsets most received "truths" about American literature; the convenient way to handle the novel, therefore, has been not to mention it at all.

When I was asked to teach an introductory course in American literature a few years ago, two standard anthologies were recommended for class use by my department, both excellent texts by scholarly editors; but when I opened them, I was surprised to find that neither editor so much as mentioned Harriet Beecher Stowe, no less included her work. Just the other day I borrowed from a colleague at The University of Connecticut a stack of freshly published anthologies, and my new tally shows still that the great majority of editors continues to rule Mrs. Stowe out of American literature. When the editors do give her a place, it is oddly the wrong one: between Emily Dickinson and Bret Harte, of all people, or heading off a section called "The Civil War."[2]

Now where does *Uncle Tom's Cabin* belong, and how are we to absorb the work into our comprehension of American literature? Here the critics should be helpful, but they turn out to be of less use than the anthologists. Richard Poirier, R. W. B. Lewis, Theodore Gross, Howard Mumford Jones, Quentin Anderson, Richard Chase — all critics who have written major studies in synthesis, works exploring the essential spirit of our literature — all present their findings about what they call *the* style, *the* spirit, *the* theory, *the* tradition, *the* heroic ideals of our literature without so much as mentioning Harriet Beecher Stowe. Even in studies of the Novel by itself — in the important work by Richard Chase, called *The American Novel and Its Tradition* — her name does not once appear.[3]

The great Edmund Wilson, who did more than any other critic to get my generation to take Harriet Beecher Stowe seriously as a writer, nevertheless insured that *Uncle Tom's Cabin* would continue to slip through the nets of lesser literary historians, because Wilson wrote of her at length in his volume devoted to the Civil War, called *Patriotic Gore*.[4] And as literature *Uncle Tom's Cabin* had nothing to do with the 1860s, the war years. Indeed, if Mrs. Stowe had divined a coming civil war, if she had suspected a coming split in the Union, she would probably never have written her first novel. The historic event that compelled her to do so was the Fugitive Slave Law of 1850, which escalated slavery into New England and remade America as a union, one nation, indivisible, with slavery and injustice for all.

Uncle Tom's Cabin was published in 1851-1852 as a serial, in 1852 as a book. Now every student of American literature knows that those years are very special ones in our cultural history; they are part of that miraculous half-decade, the early 1850s, when suddenly burst forth the most remarkable eruption of literary genius in our history (unrivaled until the 1920s, if then). In 1849-1850 appeared Emerson's *Representative Men* and Hawthorne's *The Scarlet Letter;* in 1851, Melville's *Moby-Dick;* in 1854, Thoreau's *Walden;* in 1855, Whitman's *Leaves of Grass.* Mrs. Stowe's *Uncle Tom's Cabin* came between *Moby-Dick* and *Walden,* at the center of the golden moment which F. O. Matthiessen taught us all to call, with justifiable pride, the American Renaissance. "The starting point for this book," Matthiessen wrote in the first sentence of his *American Renaissance,* "was my realization of how great a number of our past

Manuscript page from *Uncle Tom's Cabin*.

masterpieces were produced in one extraordinarily concentrated moment of expression ... the half-decade of 1850-55. ..."[5] Yet Matthiessen did not include Harriet Beecher Stowe's masterpiece. He thus offered an incomplete account of the American Renaissance, and by extension of the American literary ethos, as essentially alienated from social concerns, self-absorbed, devoted to symbolic rather than surface realities, ill at ease with novelistic plot and character, and uncertain of a reading public. None of this applies to *Uncle Tom's Cabin.* It was a different sort of work from the rest, as Harriet Beecher Stowe was different from her major contemporaries — from Emerson and Hawthorne, from Thoreau, Melville, and Whitman, who were all born within eight years, either way, of her birth date in 1811.

Harriet Beecher Stowe was different because she was a woman writer, not a man writer. As a woman writer, she was obsessed with money and work because, unlike her male contemporaries, she had to earn a living for her large family. As a woman she was concerned with "Life among the Lowly," the subtitle of *Uncle Tom's Cabin,* because she was used to hard manual labor, and she had no property rights. As a woman she was a disruptive radical, because she had nothing to gain from political patronage. As a woman she felt close ties to the literature of England and Europe, because prominent women writers of the nineteenth century made her feel at least as much at home there as here. As a woman she had no control over her place of residence (until she was in her fifties and chose to live in Hartford). But when young, a spinster daughter, she was picked up and moved and swept in the typhoon of Beecher will out West to the frontier city of Cincinnati, a city poised on two borders, between slave state and free, between East and West. Harriet Beecher Stowe was thus the only writer of the American Renaissance really to experience life in the West, really to encounter the fugitive slave before she wrote her major work. No wonder *Uncle Tom's Cabin* was different.

When we open the novel, we encounter at once a novelist sure of her public and of the power of the yarn she sets out immediately to spin. We encounter a novelist fascinated by the small differences of manner, occupation, dress, and speech which separate one regional or social species of American from another. We find that mix of pathos, comedy, and social conscience which put contemporary readers in mind of the greatest English novelist of the day, Charles Dickens (whose *David Copperfield* every literate American had been reading the year before, in 1850, just as every literate Englishman would be reading *Uncle Tom's Cabin* in 1852). But we do not at

4

**Harriet Beecher Stowe. Frontispiece for J. Cassell's first English
edition of *Uncle Tom's Cabin*.**

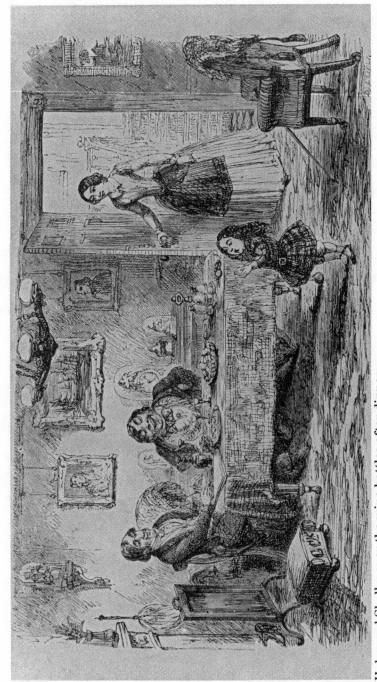

Haley and Shelby over the wine bottles after dinner.

first suspect the full sweep, the grandeur, the power of Mrs. Stowe's entire epic design. Instead we encounter a minor character whose handling is an instance of that fineness of novelistic detail which separates the work of art from the potboiler.

He is Mr. Haley, the slave trader, first of Mrs. Stowe's huge gallery of characters. Haley has none of the reputation of little Eva, Simon Legree, or Uncle Tom, those mythic figures always cited by nonreaders of *Uncle Tom's Cabin*, but he is a central and persistent feature of the novelist's design. He will keep popping up like a cork, over and over, in the current of the great river that runs through *Uncle Tom's Cabin* in order to dramatize Mrs. Stowe's central point about slavery: that it survives in America because there is money in it. And that all Americans, North or South, slave state or free, are joined in a race for the Almighty Dollar.

Mr. Haley is not remarkably cruel or bigoted, but he is universally despised — first by Mr. Shelby, the Kentucky gentleman across whose dining table Haley sits as the novel opens, there to trade in that valuable article, a slave. Shelby is a gentleman — principled, dignified, well-spoken — and Haley is not: he is the prototypical commercial traveler — thickset, coarse-featured, overdressed — with his gaudy vest and yellow-spotted blue neckerchief arranged in "a flaunting tie."

> His hands, large and coarse, were plentifully bedecked with rings; and he wore a heavy gold watch-chain, with a bundle of seals of portentous size, and a great variety of colors, attached to it, — which, in the ardor of conversation, he was in the habit of flourishing and jingling with evident satisfaction.[6]

Mr. Shelby is ashamed of having to entertain such a vulgar fellow at his own table, of having to listen to his impertinent, coarse language. But Shelby is in debt, and so must sell; Haley is in trade, and so must buy. The article of trade is a human being, and oily, persistent Haley makes the wheels of trade in flesh hum smoothly. He is an indispensable figure, the slave trader, though slaveholders as well as abolitionists hold him in abhorrence. "So long as your grand folks wants to buy men and women, I'm as good as they is," says Haley; "'tan't any meaner sellin' on 'em, than 't is buyin!"[7]

Haley's language is shot through with money, money, money; his gestures — like the jingling of those seals — speak money, money, money; even religion is money, for everything with Haley is a matter of trade. "Some folks don't believe there is pious niggers ... but *I do*. I had a fellow, now, in this yer last lot I took to Orleans — 't was as good as a meetin, now, really, to hear that critter pray; ... He

7

fetched me a good sum, too ... I realized six hundred on him. Yes, I consider religion a valeyable thing in a nigger, when it's the genuine article, and no mistake."[8]

Death, too, is part of Haley's stock in trade. When reminded that Kentucky slaves don't fancy being sold down river, because they are very likely to die on the plantations of the Delta, — "Wal, yes," Haley replies, "tol'able fast, ther dying is; what with the 'climating and one thing and another, they dies so as to keep the market up pretty brisk."[9] Nothing, not even death, is sacred; everything is a matter of trade when human beings are things to be purchased and sold. Thus, through the common character and everyday manners of trader Haley, Mrs. Stowe shows that the true horror is not the inhumanity of slavery but its very human, easygoing alignment with the normal procedures of the marketplace. "Human property is high in the market," she writes wryly in the novel,

> and is, therefore, well fed, well cleaned, tended, and looked after, that it may come to sale sleek. and strong, and shining ... and that soul immortal, once bought with blood and anguish by the Son of God ... can be sold, leased, mortgaged, exchanged for groceries or dry goods, to suit the phases of trade, or the fancy of the purchaser.[10]

One of the most poignant scenes of the novel centers around the suicide of the young slave mother, Lucy, whom Tom meets with her baby on the riverboat. Lucy throws herself in the river when she finds her baby gone, for Haley has sold the infant to a passing stranger. ("... they is raised as easy as any kind of critter there is going; they an't a bit more trouble than pups," says Haley, getting the baby's price up to forty-five dollars.) Lucy's maternal grief and Tom's reaction, as a man and a Christian, to her death make a scene in the novel that might be passed off as mere sentiment, mere propaganda, were it not for the brilliant use Mrs. Stowe makes of Haley at the end — the comedy of Haley, in which everything is money, money, money. Haley comes on deck next morning "bright and early ... to see to his live stock" and learns that this particular live item of stock, the female slave, has thrown herself overboard.

> He had seen Death many times. — met him in the way of trade, and got acquainted with him. — and he only thought of him as a hard customer ... and so he only swore that the gal was a baggage, and that he was devilish unlucky, and that, if things went on in this way, he should not make a cent on the trip. ... The trader, therefore, sat discontentedly down, with his little account-book, and put down the missing body and soul under the head of losses![11]

Lucy throws herself in the river.

CALCULATING Haley, and his money, money, money, brings to *Uncle Tom's Cabin* a strain of black comedy which belongs to a major nineteenth-century tradition. In Russia, Gogol had mastered it in a book also about the trade in human lives, called *Dead Souls.* But trader Haley is not entirely a Gogolian or even a Dickensian grotesque; he has a flat, real, down-to-earth Yankee quality, with his perpetual account-book and jingling seals. Haley even has a soul of his own, which he intends to look after in characteristic businesslike fashion: "one of these days, when I've got matters tight and snug, I calculates to tend to my soul and them ar matters...." And the moral of Haley's case requires no, and receives no, pointing up by the novelist herself, beyond the words she gives to Haley's colleague, Tom Loker: "... run up a bill with the devil all your life," snorts Loker, the slave hunter, "and then sneak out when pay time comes!"[12]

It has always seemed to me that Melville's *The Confidence-Man,* that curiously guarded satire of faith, swindling, and American commerce with the devil which Melville published five years after *Uncle Tom's Cabin*, owes something to trader Haley — owes something to Mrs. Stowe's crowd of jostling, trading, and dying passengers on a Mississippi riverboat. Surely it was Mrs. Stowe's famous novel, with its astonishingly rich river motif — its elaborate journeyings of black man and white, crisscrossing down river to hell and up river to peace and freedom — surely *Uncle Tom's Cabin* taught Melville (and Mark Twain as well) something of the symbolic resource of the Mississippi journey for American fiction.

But *Uncle Tom's Cabin* hews closer to reality than Melville's fantasy. All the journeys in the novel begin with trader Haley's deals with Mr. Shelby, over the wine bottles after dinner, when the womenfolk have left the table and it is time to trade in the real. Shelby sells Haley his best slave, Uncle Tom, and throws into the trade little Harry, Eliza and George Harris's son, "because they will bring the highest sum of any"[13] — because Tom is a good Christian and can be trusted and Harry is the brightest and lively son of exceptionally intelligent parents — because Shelby is a humane man, hates to sell more slaves than he must — because Shelby is a good family man, a good provider, has debts, must have money. How real, how humdrum, how little peculiar is the "peculiar institution" among ordinarily selfish and property-ridden Americans of the nineteenth century. No Faulknerian Gothic, no racial doom need explain the real motives of Mrs. Stowe's very real people. And the great river she sets running through *Uncle Tom's Cabin* is not only a natural force, not only a current of evil, but also Harriet

Beecher Stowe's "hurrying, foaming, tearing along" metaphor for midcentury America, for "that headlong tide of business ... poured along its wave by a race more vehement and energetic than any the old world ever saw."[14]

"But the *real* remained," Mrs. Stowe writes at one point in the novel, "the *real,* like the flat, bare, oozy tide-mud, when the blue sparkling wave ... has gone down, and there it lies, flat, slimy, bare, — exceedingly real."[15] That is not the least interesting permutation of the river symbolism which makes a literary whole of *Uncle Tom's Cabin.*

"Realism" may sound an odd label to assign to a writer of the American Renaissance, and it was in fact a new critical term, imported from French to English literary circles only in the 1850s.[16] That an aesthetic (and moral) commitment to the Real came into American literature with *Uncle Tom's Cabin* is a measure of Harriet Beecher Stowe's originality and adds a dimension to our sense of the American Renaissance, one which, however, she herself perceived in the work of her colleague, Nathaniel Hawthorne. She recommended "thorough and diligent study" of his writings to literary aspirants, for "the most commonplace object or scene, well painted by words, has an artistic value" and "the greatest artist of this sort that we have ever had in America is Hawthorne."[17]

We have forgotten that *Uncle Tom's Cabin* won its vast public here and abroad not only for its slavery matter, but also for its dedication to the American Real, its priceless evocation of the national character and daily ways. We have forgotten that the first time the phrase "The Great American Novel" was used, *Uncle Tom's Cabin* appeared to its inventor, John William DeForest, to have been the only pretender to the title, because of its "national breadth." Writing in *The Nation,* in 1868, DeForest said Mrs. Stowe's antebellum novel was the "single tale which paints American life so broadly, truly, and sympathetically that every American of feeling and culture is forced to acknowledge the picture as a likeness of something which he knows." Where other novelists failed — where Mrs. Stowe herself failed in her New England fiction — was in their narrowly regional commitments, for America in the midcentury was already a vast and varied scene; "what special interest have Southerners and Westerners and even New Yorkers in Yankee cameos?"[18]

We have forgotten that her seventeen years in frontier Cincinnati gave Harriet Beecher Stowe a sense of America as a continent, not a colony. In *Uncle Tom's Cabin* she uses the swelling waters of the River as a vantage point to look back north and east and to survey "all the broad land between the Mississippi and the Pacific. ..."[19] She sets Miss Ophelia, her quintessential Yankee spinster, on a journey to Louisiana, not only to introduce theoretical Northern abolitionism to the realities of Southern slavery, not only to oppose the rigidity and discipline of New England housekeeping to the "shiftlessness" of plantation life, but also gently to mock the narrow provincialism of the folks back east — her own people, the New Englanders.

> ... the proposal that [Ophelia] should go to Orleans was a most momentous one to the family circle. The old gray-headed father took down Morse's Atlas out of the book-case, and looked out the exact latitude and longitude; and read Flint's Travels in the South and West, to make up his own mind as to the nature of the country.

> The good mother inquired, anxiously, "if Orleans was n't an awful wicked place," saying, "that it seemed to her most equal to going to the Sandwich Islands, or anywhere among the heathen."[20]

Just as trader Haley, on the first page of the novel, serves to oppose the manners (and morals) of the commercial gent to those of the gentleman, so, further on, does Mrs. Stowe contrast the manners of the West (and their accompanying moral tone) through the "great, tall, raw-boned Kentuckians, attired in hunting-shirts, and trailing their loose joints over a vast extent of territory," who stand about the barroom of the tavern where a bill for the runaway slave, George Harris, is posted. Mrs. Stowe's Kentuckian chews tobacco and wears his hat indoors ("emblem of man's sovereignty"); he tips his chair back and stretches his long legs in the air in "an assembly of the free and easy," for —

> His fathers were mighty hunters, — men who lived in the woods, and slept under the free, open heavens, with the stars to hold their candles; and their descendant to this day always acts as if the house were his camp, — wears his hat at all hours, tumbles himself about, and puts his heels on the tops of chairs or mantelpieces, just as his father rolled on the green sward, and put his upon trees and logs, — keeps all the windows and doors open, winter and summer, that he may get air enough for his great lungs, — calls everybody "stranger," with nonchalant bonhommie, and is altogether the frankest, easiest, most jovial creature living.

"Free and easy" too is the gesture with which her Kentuckian comments on the posted handbill offering four hundred dollars for

Frederick Douglass.

Credit: National Portrait Gallery, Smithsonian Institution, Washington, D.C.

Harriet Beecher Stowe writes Frederick Douglass for guidance.

the fugitive slave, dead or alive, and including full particulars of George Harris's "very light mulatto" skin, his fine speech, his branded hand, and whip-scarred back and shoulders. "The long-legged veteran ... took down his cumbrous length, and rearing aloft his tall form, walked up to the advertisement, and very deliberately spit a full discharge of tobacco-juice on it."[21]

In manner, speech, skin color, capacity, and moral life, Mrs. Stowe distinguishes her black characters as sharply one from another as her whites, one consequence of her dedication to the American Real that has been widely misunderstood. Harriet Beecher Stowe has even come under attack by critics stubbornly ignorant of the historical "roots" that have made a complexity of black life and black families in America. In *Uncle Tom's Cabin* (and even more in *Dred,* her second slavery novel[22]) Mrs. Stowe provides extremely interesting material about the regional laws and customs, about the differing skills and trades and occupations, about the African tribal origins and American family trees that made one black American different from another in the midcentury. Harriet Beecher Stowe knew black Americans, fugitive and free, in Cincinnati; and she read the documents, many written by blacks (as her *Key to Uncle Tom's Cabin* makes clear). When *Uncle Tom's Cabin* has its due place in American literature, what today we call "black literature" will have a larger place as well. For Mrs. Stowe had in particular read Frederick Douglass, the greatest writer among black Americans up to her day; she was writing Douglass for guidance during the composition of *Uncle Tom's Cabin.*[23]

Surely she drew the character of George Harris after Frederick Douglass, for her character is an intellectual, a radical, and a leader of men; because he talks not like a darky but an educated gentleman; because he is a hired-out slave, employed at a skilled trade in a factory, not in the cotton fields — in other words, George Harris is Frederick Douglass to the life, and with many of his opinions. Mrs. Stowe knew the mind of Douglass, as did most Americans of her day, from *Narrative of the Life of Frederick Douglass, an American Slave, Written by Himself,* which Douglass published in 1845, the foundation of his fame, and the one fugitive slave narrative (out of thousands in circulation) which is unquestionably a work of literature.

Mrs. Stowe published excerpts from Douglass's *Narrative* as part of her documentation in the *Key,* where she recommends it "to anyone who has the curiosity to trace the workings of an intelligent and active mind through all the squalid misery, degradation and oppression of slavery."[24] Yet she has been attacked for falsification and even for bigotry by those ignorant of slave history in general and Douglass in particular who claim her George Harris is "really" white, not a "real" slave. She did indeed create Harris of mixed racial parentage (as was Federick Douglass), and it was another sign of her commitment to the American Real: a high proportion, probably a majority, of successful fugitives from slavery had the light skin which facilitated their escape through the Southern states. (Many wrote of passing as masters on their way through the South, as does George Harris in *Uncle Tom's Cabin;* and some of carrying off their dark-skinned friends and dependents disguised as their own slaves.[25])

Frederick Douglass made his mark, I suspect, not only on George Harris but on Mrs. Stowe's more brilliant creation of little Topsy, who just "grow'd." Every American knows about Harriet Beecher Stowe's cute pickaninny, for Topsy's words have long been part of proverbial American humor. But only readers of *Uncle Tom's Cabin,* and only those who know the full realities of childhood under slavery that Douglass's *Narrative* opened to Mrs. Stowe, can grasp the tragedy behind the comedy.

"How old are you, Topsy?" begins the famous scene. Miss Ophelia is questioning the little black slave girl bought by Augustine St. Clare for presentation to his spinster cousin from New England, and for the mutual education of both females.

> "How old are you, Topsy?"
> "Dun no, Missis," said the image, with a grin that showed all her teeth.
> "Don't know how old you are? Didn't anybody ever tell you? Who was your mother?"
> "Never had none!" said the child, with another grin.
> "Never had any mother? What do you mean? Where were you born?"
> "Never was born!" persisted Topsy. ...
> "You musn't answer me in that way, child; I'm not playing with you. Tell me where you were born, and who your father and mother were."
> "Never was born ... never had no father nor mother, nor nothin'."

Here a third voice intervenes, that of Jane — the pampered, "high yaller" house slave — who snobbishly explains to Miss Ophelia that "there's heaps of" such low Negro children: "Speculators buys 'em up cheap, when they's little, and gets 'em raised for market;" and "those low negroes, — they can't tell; they don't know anything about time ... they don't know what a year is; they don't know their own ages."[26]

Topsy and Miss Ophelia.

Douglass's autobiographical *Narrative* begins as follows: "I was born in Tuckahoe, near Hillsborough, and about twelve miles from Easton, in Talbot county, Maryland. I have no accurate knowledge of my age, never having seen any authentic record containing it." The precision, abstraction, and characteristic *hauteur* of Douglass's prose underline the appalling matter of his account. He continues:

> *By far the larger part of the slaves know as little of their ages as horses know of theirs, and it is the wish of most masters within my knowledge to keep their slaves thus ignorant. I do not remember to have ever met a slave who could tell of his birthday. They seldom come nearer to it than planting-time, harvest-time, cherry-time, spring-time, or fall-time.*

So Frederick Douglass, a man of extraordinary intellectual endowments, nevertheless also just "grow'd" — like a horse, like a plant in the fields for harvest, like Topsy.

Douglass goes on to say that he had no father, for his father was a white man, never identified, probably his master; and he had no mother, for "my mother and I were separated when I was but an infant — before I knew her as my mother. It is a common custom, in the part of Maryland from which I ran away, to part children from their mothers at a very early age."[27]

Harriet Beecher Stowe goes, however, beyond Douglass's bitterness in her Topsy scene, and beyond the Real; for the formal structure into which she fits the matter of slave birth is the catechism — those questions and answers which, for every decent white, Christian child (in Mrs. Stowe's day) marked the beginning of conscious and religious life. To Miss Ophelia, to Mrs. Stowe, the culminating horror of Topsy's slavery of ignorance is not that she knows neither her age nor human parentage, but —

> *"Have you ever heard anything about God, Topsy?"*
> *The child looked bewildered, but grinned as usual.*
> *"Do you know who made you?"*
> *"Nobody, as I knows on," said the child, with a short laugh.*
> *The idea appeared to amuse her considerably; for her eyes twinkled, and she added,*
> *"I spect I grow'd. Don't think nobody never made me."*[28]

Harriet Beecher Stowe was hardly the first Christian writer to make literature out of the catechism, as William Blake's poem reminds us:

> *Little lamb, who made thee?*
> *Dost thou know who made thee?*

To part children from their mothers was a common custom.

19

Nor was she the first American writer, for the year before *Uncle Tom's Cabin,* Hawthorne wrote a memorable catechism scene into *The Scarlet Letter.* Perhaps Mrs. Stowe built on Hawthorne — as we would surely speculate, if we were in the habit of remembering that both their first novels appeared in the early 1850s, in the "American Renaissance." His catechism scene, like Mrs. Stowe's, centers on one of the original themes of our literature: wayward, mischievous, irrepressible American youth. (Hawthorne's child is of course white and Puritan-born, while Mrs. Stowe's is black and born into slavery; but his Pearl, like her Topsy, is a girl-child.) We know, in any case, that Harriet Beecher Stowe considered *The Scarlet Letter* a work of that "natural genius" without which no amount of practice sketching everyday realities could have produced Hawthorne's masterpiece — as was, indeed, the case with her own.[29]

READERS of standard histories of American literature, even of our standard literary biographies, must assume that Nathaniel Hawthorne and Harriet Beecher Stowe were inhabitants of different planets. She was, as it happens, married to Hawthorne's Bowdoin classmate, Calvin Stowe; the Hawthornes and the Stowes met, spent a little time together, exchanged a few letters, though there was no possibility of friendship because of their opposing views on slavery. The Stowes, it need hardly be said, were staunch abolitionists; while Hawthorne, it is worth saying, regarded abolitionists as vulgar, troublemaking fanatics. His well-publicized friendship with Franklin Pierce, the compromising "locofoco" president, made Harriet Beecher Stowe regret that she had ever visited Hawthorne, though it seems not to have affected her high opinion of his writings.[30] As to Hawthorne's opinion of Mrs. Stowe's work, we can assume that he was repelled by any strong expression of antislavery views; but we should also assume that his apprehension of Mrs. Stowe as a formidable rival, his envy of her immense success with the reading public, had something to do with the hostility behind Hawthorne's often quoted animadversions on "scribbling women" — the most hostile of which date to 1851 and 1852, the *Uncle Tom's Cabin* years.[31]

Uncle Tom's Cabin is a book about American slavery in the midcentury, and *The Scarlet Letter* is not; nor is any other work by a male writer that we honor by inclusion among the major masterpieces of the American Renaissance. On the male side of our literary ledger, the avoidance of what was then (or ever) the most important social issue in America is surely a failing. On Mrs. Stowe's side it is a strength, and her choice of subject was duly honored, especially outside partisan America, by her contemporaries. "I voluntarily and sincerely veil my face," said Charlotte Brontë, "before such a mighty subject as that handled in Mrs. Beecher Stowe's work."[32]

Much is made today of Melville's "Benito Cereno," his Gothic tale about a mutiny on a Spanish slave ship in the eighteenth century — hardly pro-abolition in attitude, and in any case cautiously remote from the slavery crisis of 1856, when Melville published this tale. Far less is made of *Dred,* for few have read Mrs. Stowe's second slavery novel, also published in 1856. *Dred* deals at length, and sometimes brilliantly, with slave uprisings in the American South — close to home, and close to reality as well, for she based the novel on the story of Nat Turner (and with more fidelity to the historical records than did William Styron a few years ago).[33]

Mrs. Stowe's contemporaries were familiar with the idea, which to us sounds rather strange, that slavery was a woman's subject. They were not surprised that the most powerful response to the slavery issue in antebellum American literature was made by a woman writer, not a man. For Harriet Beecher Stowe's contemporaries knew their George Sand, their Charlotte Brontë, their Elizabeth Gaskell, their Geraldine Jewsbury, their Elizabeth Barrett Browning, their Lydia Maria Child, their Harriet Martineau. They knew that early-nineteenth-century literary women, because they were women (that is, without votes, without universities, without property, and without professions), had sensibilities alert to every species of social injustice in the world around them. However dutiful or decorous in their private lives, they had boundless resources of imaginative enthusiasm for signs of rebellion among the oppressed. In the decade preceding *Uncle Tom's Cabin,* Charlotte Brontë had written a novel about the Luddite uprisings in Yorkshire, and Mrs. Gaskell about the Chartists in Manchester, and George Sand about the secret societies that undermined the *ancien régime;* and Elizabeth Barrett Browning had written an incendiary poem about "The Runaway Slave at Pilgrim's Point."[34]

From Charles Edward Stowe's biography of his mother, we all know it was women's voices that urged her to write against slavery: sisters and sisters-in-law called out to her, "Now, Hattie, if I could use a pen as you can, I would write something that would make this whole nation feel what an accursed thing slavery is."[35] But less well-known are the women writers who preceded Harriet Beecher Stowe in the work of alerting the nation and the world to the curse of slavery. *Uncle Tom's Cabin* was not the first fugitive slave novel, only the best. Mrs. Frances Trollope had written a novel on the same subject before her; Frederika Bremer of Sweden and Harriet Martineau of England had written antislavery drama and fiction; as long before as the 1830s, Lydia Maria Child had written (and been attacked for) her *Appeal on Behalf of That Class of Americans Called Africans.*[36]

In March, 1851, Harriet Beecher Stowe wrote her historic letter to Gamaliel Bailey, editor of *The National Era,* announcing the start of *Uncle Tom's Cabin.* She wrote that she was at work upon an unusually long tale — it might fill "three or four numbers" — that would give a true picture of slavery, in her phrase, "the 'patriarchal institution.'" "I feel now that the time is come," she wrote, "when even a woman or child who can speak a word for freedom and humanity is bound to speak.... I hope every woman who can write will not be silent."[37]

Harriet Beecher Stowe was indeed a woman writer. "I wrote what I did because as a woman, as a mother, I was oppressed & broken-hearted with the sorrows of injustice I saw ...," she explained the year after *Uncle Tom's Cabin.* "I *must* speak for the oppressed — who cannot speak for themselves —"[38] *Uncle Tom's Cabin* was indeed women's literature, the "female fiction" of the American Renaissance: that is, epic in scope, bold in subject, realistic in detail, powerful in commitment to a humanitarian cause. And *Uncle Tom's Cabin* is incidentally a work of fiction unusually rich as a record of specifically female experience. The rattle and clutter of domestic life — dressing, gardening, and cooking; the household budgets, the slovenliness or precision of housekeepers, the disciplining of children and the managing of husbands — all this Mrs. Stowe recorded with a conviction rare in literature, for upon these distinctly "female matters" rested, she was convinced, the central moral issue before the nation: the perpetuation of slavery.

Eva, Topsy, Aunt Chloe, Ruth Stedman, Prue the breeder, Dinah the cook, Miss Ophelia, Jane the house slave, Lucy the suicide, Eliza Harris, Mrs. Bird: all Mrs. Stowe's immense gallery of mothers, daughters, wives, and mistresses presses into the novel to show that what women are, what women do in their "merely" domestic lives will affect the great struggle for abolition. In her famous peroration to the novel, Mrs. Stowe urged the mothers of America to *"feel right"* on the slavery issue;[39] but within the pages of the novel itself she contrived through her scenes and her characters to demonstrate that far more than right feeling was in women's power, and far more than wrong feeling was her responsibility.

Mrs. Shelby, for example, is a pious, kindly mistress to her slaves,

Harriet Beecher Stowe and daughter [Georgiana?], c. 1850-1852.

Rachel Halliday: ideal for American womanhood.

yet, for all her "right feeling" she is as responsible as her husband for the sale of Uncle Tom, because of her ignorance of her husband's debts, her unwitting acquiescence in plantation extravagance. And Marie St. Clare, though a cruel and selfish slave mistress, is less to be blamed for her "wrong feeling" (to which, as a Southern belle, she was reared) than for her frigidity as a wife, whose coldness saps her husband's will and makes St. Clare's abhorrence of Louisiana slavery all a matter of intellect, not action.

One character in *Uncle Tom's Cabin*, Rachel Halliday, was clearly intended to represent Harriet Beecher Stowe's ideal for American womanhood. She is the Quaker mother whose serene, orderly, abundant domestic paradise in Indiana is also a principal way station on the Underground Railroad. But it is not so much Rachel's Quaker faith or even her antislavery activism that Mrs. Stowe holds up, rather wistfully, to our admiring gaze, but instead her maternal skills. For Rachel has an enviable technique, beyond price in a society lacking in servants either slave or free, for eliciting, without nagging, the voluntary performance of domestic chores by

> busy girls and boys ... who all moved obediently to Rachel's gentle "Thee had better," or more gentle "Hadn't thee better?" in the work of getting breakfast; for a breakfast in the luxurious valleys of Indiana is a thing complicated and multiform, and, like picking up the rose-leaves and trimming the bushes in Paradise, asking other hands than those of the original mother.[40]

When all Mrs. Stowe's letters have been published, and new biographical studies written about the whole human being she was, we shall see that her celebration of order, serenity, and discipline in a woman's domestic life did not come easily or automatically. She herself was no Rachel Halliday — no effortless manager, no Christian queen of a servantless household of seven children; no woman is. There was something of the sloven and the shrew, the neurotic and the rebel, the whiner, the spendthrift, the addlepate, and the failure in Harriet Beecher Stowe as wife and mother; as there is in every woman. Her real struggles as daughter and stepdaughter (half angelic little Eva, half impish Topsy), as romantic adolescent, ambitious young writer, and awkward bride, as overwhelmed housekeeper, and frantic mother, will make her more real to us as a person,[41] and lead us to take a more serious interest in her writings about womanhood — a state of being which she regarded as immensely difficult, and immensely important.

Her kind of feminism was the feminism of the Victorian wife and mother. It has gone quite out of fashion, may never come back into fashion again, and there are many reasons, some of them pointed out by Mark Twain, to find it unattractive. "But I reckon I got to light out for the Territory ahead of the rest," says Huck Finn at the end of Mark Twain's novel, "because Aunt Sally she's going to adopt and sivilize me and I can't stand it. I been there before."

Harriet Beecher Stowe had, however, "been there before" herself, and half a century ahead of *Huckleberry Finn.* Her Tom Loker, the slave hunter in *Uncle Tom's Cabin,* becomes a changed man after being nursed back to health by Quaker womenfolk. "Nice people," he will henceforth say of the Quakers; "wanted to convert me, but couldn't come it, exactly." Somewhat like Huck, Tom lights out for "the new settlements" and "in place of slave-catching . . . his talents developed themselves more happily in trapping bears, wolves, and other inhabitants of the forest. . . ."[42]

Notes

1. Edward Wagenknecht, *Harriet Beecher Stowe: The Known and the Unknown* (New York: Oxford University Press, 1965), p. 16; Forrest Wilson, *Crusader in Crinoline: The Life of Harriet Beecher Stowe* (Philadelphia: J. B. Lippincott Company, 1941), pp. 325-330; Edmund Wilson, *Patriotic Gore: Studies in the American Civil War* (New York: Oxford University Press, 1962), pp. 3-11; Harriet Beecher Stowe, Introduction to the New Edition of *Uncle Tom's Cabin* (Cambridge: Riverside Press of Houghton, Mifflin & Co., 1878), *passim*. For the many detailed studies in English and in most other languages of the foreign response to *Uncle Tom's Cabin,* see Margaret Holbrook Hildreth, *Harriet Beecher Stowe: A Bibliography* (Hamden: Archon Books, 1976), *passim*. One of the most recent and best of these studies is James Woodress, "Uncle Tom's Cabin in Italy," *Essays on American Literature in Honor of Jay B. Hubbell,* ed. Clarence Gohdes (Durham: Duke University Press, 1967), pp. 126-140. Professor Woodress details the unbroken Italian interest from 1852 to the 1960s, shown through the one hundred editions and reprints, and the translations by many hands up to recent years, and comments: "It is probably safe to say that every Italian with a high school education has read the book. In view of the novel's vogue in Italy, it comes as a surprise to Italians to learn that the book is not so well known in the United States. An American professor is fortunate if half of the students in his undergraduate survey course in American literature have read *Uncle Tom's Cabin,* and it is a rare college course in which the novel is required or collateral reading." (p. 127).

2. A notable exception to the rule of omission in recent anthologies is *Literature in America* (New York: Free Press, 1971), of which the general editor is Edward Wagenknecht, the author of *Harriet Beecher Stowe: The Known and the Unknown,* one of the best books about Mrs. Stowe, and of *Cavalcade of the American Novel* (New York: Holt, 1952), in which due place is given her contribution to American fiction (chap. v). In volume II of Wagenknecht's anthology (ed. Donald Hausdorff) a well chosen selection, correctly located, from *Uncle Tom's Cabin* (chap. XXX, "The Slave Warehouse") is included. The importance of anthologies cannot be overestimated, for they establish the perimeters today of what little students know of our literature.

3. Richard Poirier, *A World Elsewhere: The Place of Style in American Literature* (1966); R. W. B. Lewis, *The American Adam* (1955) and *Trials of the Word* (1965); Theodore Gross, *The Heroic Ideal in American Literature* (1971); Howard Mumford Jones, *The Theory of American Literature* (1948); Quentin Anderson, *The Imperial Self* (1971); and Richard Chase, *The American Novel and Its Tradition* (1957). For an account of the fame of *Uncle Tom's Cabin* inside academia, see Jay B. Hubbell, *Who Are the Major American Writers?: A Study of the Changing Literary Canon* (Durham: Duke University Press, 1972), pp. 88, 94, 97, 102, 265, 289, 300, 307.

4. Edmund Wilson, *Patriotic Gore,* pp. 3-58. Wilson's influence began much earlier with his November 27, 1948, *New Yorker* article occasioned by the Modern Library Edition of *Uncle Tom's Cabin,* in which he wrote, as has almost every critic after him, "To come to 'Uncle Tom' for the first time today may, therefore, be a startling experience. It is a much more

remarkable book than one has ever been allowed to suspect." (p. 134).

5. F. O. Matthiessen, *American Renaissance: Art and Expression in the Age of Emerson and Whitman* (New York: Oxford University Press, 1941), p. vii.
6. Harriet Beecher Stowe, *Uncle Tom's Cabin; or, Life among the Lowly,* ed. Kenneth S. Lynn (Cambridge: Belknap Press of Harvard University, 1962), p. 5, chap. I. All subsequent citations are to this edition, with chapters indicated to facilitate reference to other editions.
7. *Uncle Tom's Cabin,* p. 106, chap. X.
8. *Uncle Tom's Cabin,* p. 6, chap. I.
9. *Uncle Tom's Cabin,* p. 104, chap. X.
10. *Uncle Tom's Cabin,* p. 334, chap. XXX.
11. *Uncle Tom's Cabin,* pp. 133-137, chap. XII.
12. *Uncle Tom's Cabin,* p. 71, chap. VIII.
13. *Uncle Tom's Cabin,* p. 37, chap. V.
14. *Uncle Tom's Cabin,* p. 148, chap. XIV.
15. *Uncle Tom's Cabin,* pp. 159-160, chap. XV.
16. The first English use of the word "realism" was in an anonymous article on "Balzac and His Writings" in the July, 1853, *Westminster Review,* edited by then Mary Ann Evans (later George Eliot); see Richard Stang, *The Theory of the Novel in England: 1850-1870* (London: Routledge and Kegan Paul, 1959), pp. 148-149 and the chapter "Realism with a Difference," pp. 159-176. For Mrs. Stowe's influence on George Eliot, see my *Literary Women* (Garden City: Doubleday & Company, Inc., 1976), pp. 38-39, 43, 46-47.
17. Harriet Beecher Stowe, "How Shall I Learn To Write?," *Hearth and Home,* January 16, 1869, p. 56. In this article, part of a series, Harriet Beecher Stowe recommended that the aspiring writer study Hawthorne's exercises in capturing everyday realities (digging potatoes, pigs at Brook Farm, a little seamstress, an old apple dealer, etc.) in *Passages from the American Note-Books of Nathaniel Hawthorne,* published by Ticknor & Fields in 1868. See notes 29 and 30.
18. John William DeForest, "The Great American Novel," *The Nation,* January 9, 1868, pp. 27-29. (I am grateful to Professor Thomas P. Riggio of The University of Connecticut for keeping me from forgetting this article.) DeForest had published *Miss Ravenel's Conversion,* his own notable first novel, in 1867.
19. *Uncle Tom's Cabin,* p. 75, chap. VIII and p. 149, chap. XIV.
20. *Uncle Tom's Cabin,* pp. 162-163, chap. XV.
21. *Uncle Tom's Cabin,* pp. 108-110, chap. XI.
22. For a discussion of *Dred* as a repository of authentic black history and literature, see my article, "Mrs. Stowe's Vengeance," *The New York Review of Books,* September 3, 1970, pp. 25-32.
23. Harriet Beecher Stowe to Frederick Douglass, July 9, 1851, in Charles Edward Stowe, *Life of Harriet Beecher Stowe Compiled from Her Letters and Journals* (Boston: Houghton, Mifflin and Company, 1889), pp. 149-153.
24. Harriet Beecher Stowe, *A Key to Uncle Tom's Cabin* (Leipzig: Tauchnitz, 1853), vol. I, pp. 38-46, chap. IV ("George Harris"). For Douglass's tributes to the authenticity as well as the power of Mrs. Stowe's slavery fiction, see *Life and Writings of Frederick Douglass,* ed. Philip Foner

(New York: International Publishers, 1950), vol. II, pp. 226-228, 240-242, 356.

25. See Gilbert Osofsky, Introduction to *Puttin' on Ole Massa* (New York: Harper & Row, 1969), pp. 19, 28. The most thrilling historical account of such an escape through racial disguise, in which the light-skinned wife dressed as a planter, her husband accompanying her in the guise of her slave, is *Running a Thousand Miles for Freedom, or The Escape of William and Ellen Craft from Slavery* in *Great Slave Narratives*, ed. Arna Bontemps (Boston: Beacon Press, 1969), pp. 269-314. See note 22.
26. *Uncle Tom's Cabin*, pp. 246-247, chap. XX.
27. Frederick Douglass, *Narrative of the Life of Frederick Douglass, an American Slave, Written by Himself*, ed. Benjamin Quarles (Cambridge: Belknap Press of Harvard University Press, 1960), pp. 23-24.
28. *Uncle Tom's Cabin*, p. 247, chap. XX.
29. In a later article in the series on writing cited in note 17, Harriet Beecher Stowe wrote, "if Hawthorne had not had a natural genius for writing, do you suppose keeping a journal ... would have only made him an insufferable, hum-drum plodder. ..." ("How Do I Know That I Can Make a Writer?," *Hearth and Home*, January 30, 1869, p. 88. See notes 30 and 31.)
30. On November 3, 1863, Harriet Beecher Stowe wrote to James T. Fields (who was her own as well as Hawthorne's publisher), "Do tell me if our friend Hawthorne praises that arch traitor Pierce in his preface & your loyal firm publishes it — I never read the preface & have not yet seen the book but they say so here & I can scarcely believe it of you — if I can of him — I regret that I went to see him last summer — What! patronize such a traitor to our faces!" The Hawthorne book in question, indeed dedicated to Pierce, was *Our Old Home* (1863), impressions of England gleaned during Hawthorne's four-year term as Liverpool consul, a highly lucrative post he owed to the patronage of President Franklin Pierce, a Bowdoin classmate and lifelong friend, whose campaign biography Hawthorne had written. Loyalty, gratitude, and affection inspired the dedication to the antiabolitionist ex-president; but it worried Fields and offended not only abolitionists but also most Northerners, for the Civil War was then in progress and Pierce urged its cessation. (See Randall Stewart, *Nathaniel Hawthorne: A Biography* [New Haven: Yale University Press, 1948], pp. 132-133, 179, 230-233.) The female abolitionist with whom Hawthorne had debated over the years with particular vehemence was his sister-in-law, the redoubtable educator, reformer, and editor, Elizabeth Peabody, who commented years later that Hawthorne wrote the dedication to Pierce not only over her protests but also "to antagonize what he was zaney enough to call my fanaticism." (Elizabeth P. Peabody to Mrs. Harriet M. Lothrop, September, 1887, *Nathaniel Hawthorne Journal*, 1972, p. 7.)

The Harriet Beecher Stowe letter to Fields, which has never been printed in its entirety, is quoted with the permission of the Huntington Library, San Marino, California, as are other letters to Fields cited later. The letter opens with a long enthusiastic rattle about the progress of Mrs. Stowe's first Hartford home (Oakholm), then a-building, including the phrase: "my house with *eight* gables is growing wonderfully" — perhaps, in view of the Hawthorne outburst that follows, a little boast that she was going one better than the author of *The House of the Seven Gables*. Two years later, however, she thanked Fields for the handsomely bound set of Hawthorne's works that he presented to her daughter as a wedding present: "Nothing could be prettier, more [lastingly?] beautiful — the first adjective belonging you observe to the getting up — the second to the contents." (May 18, 1865; Huntington Library.) And in 1869 she wrote for publication the praise of Hawthorne's genius cited in note 29.

31. By all accounts, *Uncle Tom's Cabin* took the nation by storm during its run as a serial in *The National Era* (June 5, 1851, to April 1, 1852) and the book, published by Jewett on March 20, 1852, was selling at the rate of ten thousand copies a week by July; conservative estimates of total sales in America and England were a million copies by the end of 1852, with English estimates of a million copies in that country alone, where sales were if anything brisker, unhampered by antiabolitionist prejudice or the need to pay Mrs. Stowe royalties. Every author, and virtually every literate person, was aware of the book's immense success by the end of 1852. On December 11, 1852, Hawthorne wrote to Fields: "*All* women, as authors, are feeble and tiresome. I wish they were forbidden to write, on pain of having their faces deeply scarified with an oyster-shell." (Huntington Library.) Hawthorne's more often quoted "d———d mob of scribbling women" letter to Fields dates to 1855 and makes clear that the competitive threat posed by women's novels underlay his hostility. "Worse they could not be, and better they need not be," Hawthorne wrote of female novels, "when they sell by the 100,000." Similar competitive outbursts can be found among male English novelists; and it should be remembered that the 1840s and the 1850s saw the publication by women not only of trashy best sellers but also of masterpieces of fiction that reached a wide public. (See Frank Luther Mott, *Golden Multitudes: The Story of Best Sellers in the United States* [New York: The Macmillan Company, 1947], p. 122; my "Bleak House: The Agitating Women," *The Dickensian*, January, 1973, pp. 22-24; E. Bruce Kirkham, *The Building of Uncle Tom's Cabin* [Knoxville: University of Tennessee Press, 1977], p. 192.)

32. Charlotte Brontë to George Smith, October 30, 1852, in *The Brontës: Their Lives, Friendships and Correspondence*, ed. T. J. Wise and J. A. Symington (Oxford: Shakespeare Head Press, 1932), vol. IV, p. 14.

33. See my article cited in note 22 and the subsequent exchange of letters with William Styron, who indicated he had read Harriet Beecher Stowe's "neglected work," *Dred*. (*The New York Review of Books*, November 19, 1970.)

34. Charlotte Brontë, *Shirley* (1849); Elizabeth Gaskell, *Mary Barton* (1848); George Sand, *Consuelo* (1842-1843) and its continuation, *La Comtesse de Rudolstadt* (1843-1844); Elizabeth Barrett Browning, "The Runaway Slave at Pilgrim's Point" (1848).

35. Charles Edward Stowe, *Life of Harriet Beecher Stowe*, p. 145.

36. Frances Trollope, *Jonathan Jefferson Whitlaw* (1836); Frederika Bremer, *The Bondmaid* (translated, 1844) and, for her prediction, made during her American tour, that great fiction about the fugitive slave

would be made by "noble-minded American women, American mothers who have hearts and genius," see Charles H. Foster, *The Rungless Ladder: Harriet Beecher Stowe and New England Puritanism* (Durham: Duke University Press, 1954), p. 57; Harriet Martineau, *The Hour and the Man* (1841); Lydia Maria Child, *Appeal on Behalf of That Class of Americans Called Africans* (1833) and, for her punishment, see my *Literary Women*, p. 283.

37. Harriet Beecher Stowe to Gamaliel Bailey, March 9, 1851, in Joseph S. Van Why, *Nook Farm*, ed. Earl A. French (Hartford: The Stowe-Day Foundation, 1975), pp. 16-18. Mrs. Stowe goes on in the letter to cite the literary woman who today we would call a "role model" — "I have admired and sympathized with the fearless and free spirit of Grace Greenwood, and her letters have done my heart good." Once famous, now forgotten, Grace Greenwood was, like Mrs. Stowe, of New England Puritan stock (a descendant of Jonathan Edwards), who earned her way, as did Mrs. Stowe, as a popular writer of poems, essays, and journalism. She also worked as an editorial assistant on *Godey's Lady's Book,* until the antislavery letters she contributed in 1850 to *The National Era* offended *Godey's* Southern subscribers — and cost Grace Greenwood her job. These are the letters which, Harriet Beecher Stowe wrote, "have done my heart good." (Barbara Welter on Grace Greenwood, *Notable American Women: A Biographical Dictionary* [Cambridge: Belknap Press of Harvard University Press, 1974], vol. II, pp. 407-409.)

38. Harriet Beecher Stowe to Lord Chief Justice Denman, January 20, 1853. (Huntington Library.)

39. *Uncle Tom's Cabin,* p. 57, chap. XLV.

40. *Uncle Tom's Cabin,* p. 145, chap. XIII.

41. My own sense of a more complex person comes from examination of her unpublished letters in the Huntington Library and the Schlesinger Library of Radcliffe College. For an authoritative account of the partial and imperfect publication to date of Mrs. Stowe's letters, see E. Bruce Kirkham, "Harriet Beecher Stowe: Autobiography and Legend," *Portraits of a Nineteenth Century Family: A Symposium on the Beecher Family,* ed. Earl A. French and Diana Royce (Hartford: The Stowe-Day Foundation, 1976), pp. 51-69.

42. *Uncle Tom's Cabin,* p. 393, chap. XXXVII. The Mark Twain line is the concluding sentence of *Adventures of Huckleberry Finn.*

Epigraphs

William Dean Howells, *My Literary Passions,* Library Edition of *The Writings of William Dean Howells* (New York: Harper & Bros., 1895), p. 50.

Lev N. Tolstoi, *What Is Art?, Works by Count Lev N. Tolstoi,* trans. Leo Wiener (Boston: Colonial Press, 1904-1912), vol. XXII, pp. 299-300.

Anthony Burgess, "Making de White Boss Frown," *Encounter,* July 1966, pp. 54-55.

A Note on Mark Twain
and
Harriet Beecher Stowe

Mark Twain, c. 1860-1870. Note misspelling of S. L. Clemens.

Harriet Beecher Stowe, c. 1869-1872.

BORN in 1835, Samuel Langhorne Clemens was twenty-four years younger than Harriet Beecher Stowe. But the major fiction of Mark Twain, *The Adventures of Tom Sawyer* and *Adventures of Huckleberry Finn,* was published rather late, when he was in his forties and fifties — that is, the 1870s and 1880s, his Connecticut years, when he was closest geographically and, for want of a better word, literarily to Mrs. Stowe. Mark Twain in fact moved to Hartford's Nook Farm in 1871 *because* it was an enclave of Beechers, the family which then represented to him all that was best in American religion, morality, prosperous domesticity, and literary professionalism. "I never saw any place where morality and huckleberries flourished as they do here," he commented on his first sight of Hartford.[1]

It was in 1868 that Mark Twain first met Harriet Beecher Stowe, Henry Ward Beecher, Isabella Beecher Hooker, and other members of that enormous family. He was staying in New York and Brooklyn, fresh from his *Quaker City* cruise and beginning to be talked about as the journalist from California who made everyone laugh with his story about a jumping frog. Later that same year, 1868, he first visited Hartford as a guest of John and Isabella Beecher Hooker, whose house on Forest Street he would rent in 1871 after his marriage to Olivia Langdon (the marriage performed in Elmira, New York, by Thomas K. Beecher).

The Harriet Beecher Stowe that Mark Twain met in 1868 was at the peak of her national fame as a writer. (It was the year that John William DeForest praised her as the author of "The Great American Novel" in *The Nation.*) In the decade between *Uncle Tom's Cabin* and the Civil War, she had written about a book a year: *A Key to Uncle Tom's Cabin, Sunny Memories of Foreign Lands, Dred, The*

Minister's Wooing, The Pearl of Orr's Island, Agnes of Sorrento.
During the war years she wrote mainly journalism, having become
a starring contributor to *The Atlantic Monthly,* the *summa* of
American magazines from its founding in 1857. Her literary
prosperity made possible the building in 1863-1864 of Oakholm, her
elaborate Nook Farm dream house "with *eight* gables," as she
boasted.[2] Oakholm proved too extravagant (as did all the Nook
Farm houses) and in 1873 the Stowes moved to a more modest
cottage on Forest Street — the delightful Stowe house we visit
today. To see how far away the Clemens family then lived — in the
house they were renting from the Hookers — the visitor should turn
right upon leaving the front door of the Stowe house and walk down
the street to the corner of Forest and Hawthorn Streets; then across
Forest Street to have a look at the enormous turreted pile set back
from the sidewalk. (Turned into apartments, the house is not open to
the public.)

In the post-Civil War years Mrs. Stowe did her best work as a
stylist of American prose, in the two books which some consider her
masterpieces: *Oldtown Folks* (1869) and its successor, *Sam Law-
son's Oldtown Fireside Stories* (1873). These two works we know
Mark Twain read with care and valued for their realism, dialect
humor, nostalgia for childhood, and regional authenticity — a
literary mix for which she was the principal American pioneer, he
the brilliant follower.[3]

In the same years Mark Twain's first full-length works, *The
Innocents Abroad* (1869), *Roughing It* (1872), and *The Gilded Age*
(1873), furthered his reputation as a humorist from the Southwest,
but part of the point of taking up residence in Connecticut was that
he should establish himself more seriously in the center of American letters, which then still meant New England, and specifically
meant publication in *The Atlantic Monthly.* He achieved the latter
for the first time in 1874 with "A True Story" (which ran in the
November *Atlantic*): a sketch for which Professor William Gibson
makes large claims in his recent study of *The Art of Mark Twain.*
The sketch purports to be a faithful transcription, "Word for Word
as I Heard It," of the life story of the Clemens's black cook: a former
slave mother all of whose children were sold away from her, save
one son whom she lost and then recovered during the Civil War.
(There is no evidence that Mark Twain read Harriet Beecher
Stowe's *Dred,* but anyone who has done so will be reminded of its
most brilliant chapter, "Milly's Story," the one selection from her
work that should be in every anthology of American literature.)[4]

The same year, 1874, Mark Twain and Harriet Beecher Stowe

Oakholm, c. 1865. Harriet Beecher Stowe's eight-gabled dreamhouse.

The Hooker House, Mark Twain's first Hartford home, c. 1883.

became backyard neighbors when he moved into his newly built home on Farmington Avenue around the corner — the magnificent establishment visitors tour today. (Its conservatory reputedly owed something to Mrs. Stowe's ideas on home decoration.) And after Mark Twain joined Harriet Beecher Stowe as a regular contributor to *The Atlantic Monthly,* they were from time to time periodical neighbors in *The Atlantic* just as they were across-the-lawn neighbors in Nook Farm. To all visitors to Hartford, then as now,[5] they were the two great literary lions of the place.

Outside of Hartford, however, Mrs. Stowe's national prestige suffered a permanent blow at the start of the 1870s, when she espoused the cause of the late Lady Byron (whom she had met in England) and wrote from a Victorian wife's point of view the story of her separation from the poet, alluding for the first time in print to Byron's incestuous relationship with his half sister. Mrs. Stowe's "The True Story of Lady Byron's Life" ran in *The Atlantic* in 1869, caused a storm, hurt circulation, and ushered in her period of feminist writings: the full-length *Lady Byron Vindicated* (1870), *My Wife and I* (1871), *Pink and White Tyranny* (1871), and *We and Our Neighbors* (1875). The last three are her lightweight, semi-polemical, semi-society novels on the marriage and wife-style question. I find them informative and enjoyable, but whatever their literary and feminist vices or virtues, they certainly show that Harriet Beecher Stowe retained all her mental vigor and professional spirit during the 1870s, while Mark Twain was writing *Tom Sawyer* (published in 1876) and beginning, with starts and stops, *Adventures of Huckleberry Finn* (published in 1884).

Mark Twain was also caught up in the feminist agitation that swept through Nook Farm in the 1870s, and, oddly enough, here he and Harriet Beecher Stowe came closest together in their views. Both were proponents of, though not fighters for, women suffrage.[6] But the specific issue that drew them together, and split them both from Isabella Beecher Hooker, was the Henry Ward Beecher adultery trial in the mid-1870s. Mrs. Hooker, with the radical feminists on her side, asserted Beecher's guilt, the two novelists his innocence. Lasting reminders of their mutual loyalty and devotion to the celebrated minister are the portrait of Beecher which dominates the front parlor of the Stowe house and his marble bust in the foyer of the Mark Twain house.[7]

They exchanged their books and made gifts of them to each other's children; they were of course aware of each other's writing, especially as both wrote increasingly out of childhood reminiscence. Mrs. Stowe's last novel, *Poganuc People* (1878), handled with

Mark Twain House, c. 1875.

Harriet Beecher Stowe House, c. 1875-1882.

warmth and humor her New England childhood in a minister's household; it surely owed some inspiration to *Tom Sawyer*. (The two books make interesting companion pieces for comparing growing up male with growing up female in antebellum America.)

As to the antislavery matter which figures with such fascinating ambivalence in Mark Twain's novels of boyhood, it should be remembered that he was born a Southerner in Missouri, a border state, and had elected to skirmish briefly as a Rebel during the Civil War (when he was in his late twenties, and other of his relatives chose the Union side). The best comment on Tom Sawyer's harebrained scheme to rescue Nigger Jim from slavery was made by Mark Twain himself, in a quip he gave to Huck Finn: "It don't seem right and fair that Harriet Beacher Stow and all them other second-handers gets all the credit of starting that war and you never hear Tom Sawyer mentioned in the histories."[8]

Calvin Stowe died in 1886, and from then on Mrs. Stowe behaved like an old lady — as she was entitled to do, for she was seventy-five. But she was still up to reading Mark Twain — congratulating him on *The Prince and the Pauper* with a fervor that brought tears to his eyes[9] — and to supervising the work on her biography in a manner that shows that she was hardly senile — an adjective too often applied to her entire Nook Farm period by those who have only the vaguest knowledge of her career. She probably suffered a stroke as she neared eighty, and she died at eighty-five in 1896, but by then Nook Farm, as a major literary colony, was no more. Mark Twain was already a wandering resident of Europe, forced by his financial troubles to abandon in 1891 his costly Nook Farm establishment.

"I never saw any place where morality and huckleberries flourished as they do here," he exclaimed years before of Hartford. According to Mark Twain's biographer, Justin Kaplan, the purplish, tart-sweet, little berries were unknown in Missouri in his youth; he saw huckleberries growing and picked for the first time on his 1868 visit to Hartford. As his choice of a name of his boy of the West, "Huckleberry" should remind us of his choice of New England as literary residence; and that Mark Twain became a national, rather than a merely regional, figure when he settled down among the Connecticut Beechers. Visitors to Nook Farm should go first to the female cottage on Forest Street and second to the great masculine *palazzo* on Farmington Avenue; for in every historical sense that matters here — from decoration to literature, from huckleberries to morality — Harriet Beecher Stowe came first to Nook Farm.

Notes

1. Justin Kaplan, *Mr. Clemens and Mark Twain: A Biography* (New York: Simon and Schuster, 1966), p. 64.
2. See note 30 after "Harriet Beecher Stowe and American Literature."
3. Alan Gribben, The Library and Reading of Samuel L. Clemens (Berkeley: University of California, 1974), pp. 1932-1933. Ph.D. dissertation. The pages referring to Harriet Beecher Stowe are available in The Stowe-Day Library. See also Albert E. Stone, Jr., *The Innocent Eye: Childhood in Mark Twain's Imagination* (New Haven: Yale University Press, 1961), p. 9; and Walter Blair, *Mark Twain and Huck Finn* (Berkeley; University of California Press, 1960), pp. 111-112.
4. William M. Gibson, *The Art of Mark Twain* (New York: Oxford University Press, 1976), pp. 76-80, 124; Mark Twain, "A True Story, Repeated Word for Word as I Heard It," *The Atlantic Monthly* (November, 1874), pp. 591-594; Harriet Beecher Stowe, "Milly's Story," *Dred: A Tale of the Great Dismal Swamp,* vol. I, chap. XVI (Boston: Phillips, Sampson and Company, 1856).
5. Kenneth R. Andrews, *Nook Farm: Mark Twain's Hartford Circle* (Cambridge: Harvard University Press, 1950), p. 130. During the 1883 Hartford fair Harriet Beecher Stowe and Mark Twain stood side by side autographing books and led a costume march at a "Carnival of Authors." This trivial episode is notable because of its late date, 1883; it should serve to counteract the impression, furthered by innumerable biographers, that Mrs. Stowe was a nonentity or a senile lunatic throughout Mark Twain's Nook Farm years.
6. For the similarity of their views in favor of woman suffrage, compare Harriet Beecher Stowe, "What Is and What Is Not the Point in the Woman Question," *Hearth and Home* (August 28, 1869), pp. 568-569; and Mark Twain, "The Temperance Crusade and Woman's Rights," in *Europe and Elsewhere,* Stormfield Edition of *Mark Twain's Works* (New York: Harper & Brothers, 1929), pp. 24-30.
7. Kenneth R. Andrews, *Nook Farm*, pp. 35-39. See p. 52 for Mark Twain's classic "sexist" comment on Beecher's alleged adultery: "What a pity — that so insignificant a matter as the chastity or unchastity of an Elizabeth Tilton could clip the locks of this Sampson. ..."
8. Mark Twain, "Tom Sawyer's Conspiracy," quoted in Alan Gribben, The Library and Reading of Mark Twain, p. 1935.
9. Justin Kaplan, *Mark Twain*, p. 240.

Ellen Moers is the author of *Literary Women*, *Two Dreisers*, and *The Dandy: Brummell to Beerbohm*. Her articles on English, French, and American literature have appeared in *The New York Review of Books*, *The New York Times Book Review*, *The American Scholar*, *Commentary*, *Harper's*, *Victorian Studies*, and other journals. Often invited to lecture by universities and societies here and abroad, Dr. Moers presented the lecture upon which this book is based to The Stowe-Day Foundation while she was Visiting University Professor at the University of Connecticut in 1976.

Credit: Alex Gotfryd

". . . in America we are not in the habit of speculating on the literary consequences of *Uncle Tom's Cabin,* only the historical. We think of *Uncle Tom's Cabin* as belonging to American history—and *Huckleberry Finn* to American literature. My intention is to put *Uncle Tom's Cabin* back in American literature where it belongs. . . ."

The Stowe-Day Foundation
77 Forest Street
Hartford, Connecticut 06105

ISBN: 0-917482-15-8